boca

esófago

...ado

...lon

...éndice

estómago

intestino
grueso

recto

mouth ·········

esophagus

liver

colon

appendix

stom

larg

intest

rect

The Long Journey of Mister Poop
El Gran Viaje del Señor Caca

Angèle Delaunois

Marie Lafrance

Translated by Daniel Zolinsky

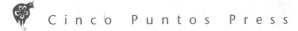
Cinco Puntos Press

¡Ah, una hermosa

manzani

roja!

¡Qué
sabroso es
morderla

Ohhh, what a beautiful little red apple! It will be so lovely to bite into it!

¡Vamos dientes!

¡A trabajar!

Introduces los alimentos en tu boca y los mezclas con saliva.

Now, put the food in your mouth where it will mix with your saliva.

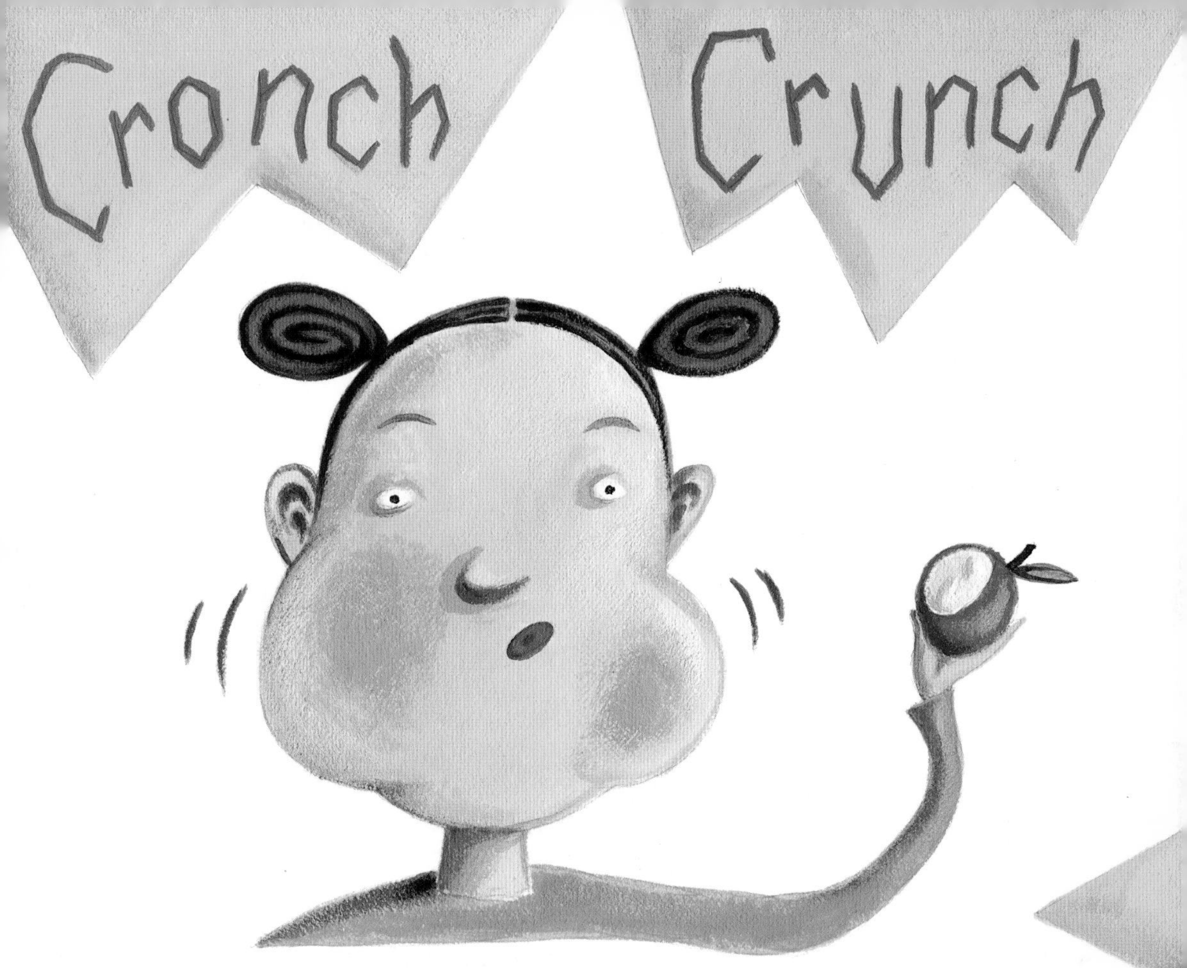

All right, teeth!

Get to work!

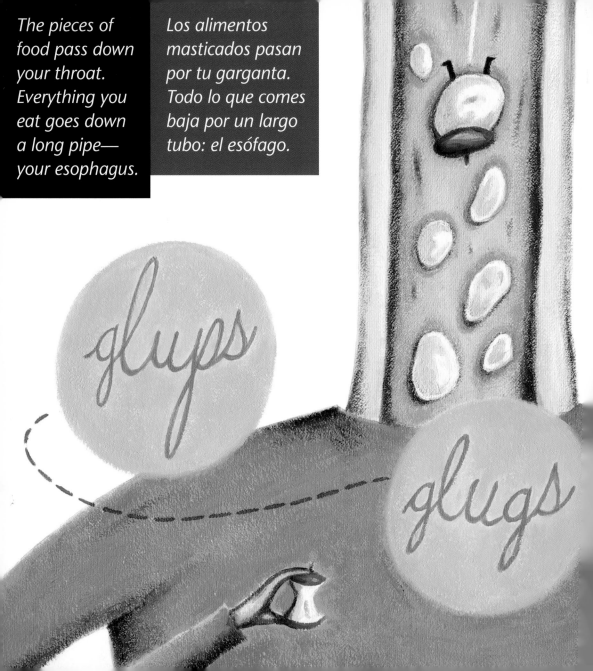

The pieces of food pass down your throat. Everything you eat goes down a long pipe—your esophagus.

Los alimentos masticados pasan por tu garganta. Todo lo que comes baja por un largo tubo: el esófago.

glups

glugs

Hey, don't swallow so fast!—
you'll
choke!

No tragues tan rápido!
¡Te puedes
atragantar!

Look out, everybody!

We're going to stir the vegetables!

Los alimentos llegan al estómago. Todo lo que tragas, él lo digiere.

The food arrives in your stomach. It must digest everything that you swallow.

The acids and enzymes change the texture of the foods.

Los ácidos y las enzimas modifican la textura de los alimentos.

Es la fábrica.
Todo se ha transformado en papilla.

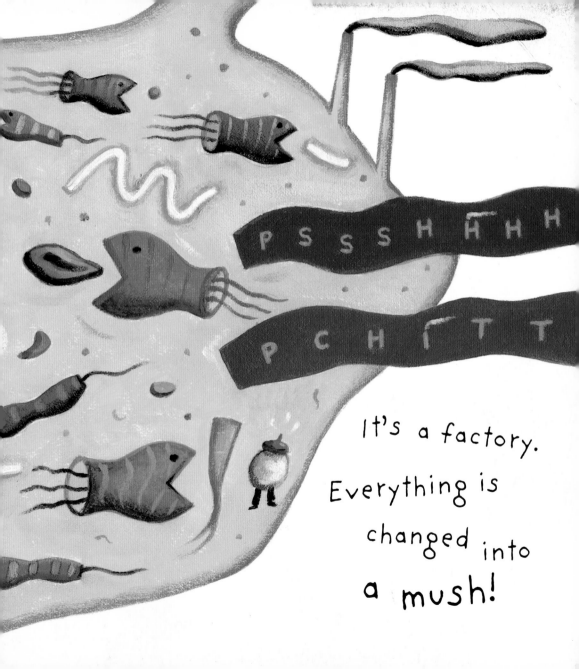

Your liver makes bile which helps digestion.

Tu hígado hace la bilis para ayudar a la digestión.

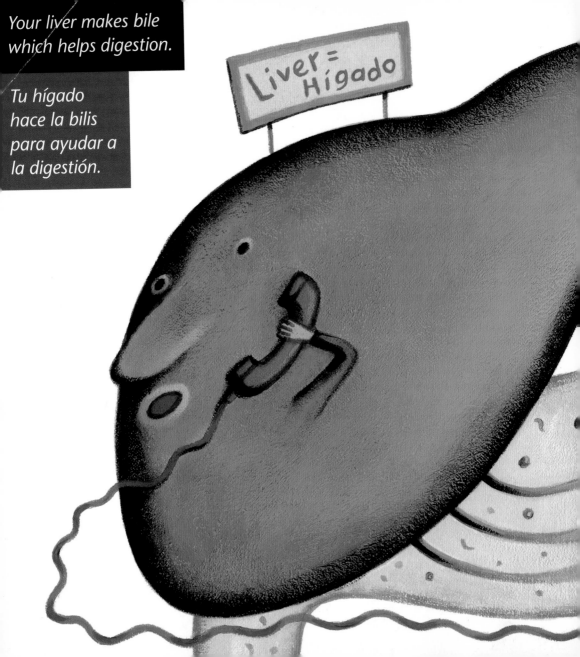

Liver = Hígado

¿Hola, hablo con el hígado?

¡Necesitamos ayuda!

Hello, Liver?

We need help!

La papilla baja hasta el intestino delgado y puede quedarse ahí varios días.

¡Otro tubo más! Pero éste es superlargo.

The mush goes down to your small intestine and can stay there for several days.

Another pipe, already?!
This one is really long!

Your blood's red corpuscles come into the mush to find everything they need so that you can stay healthy.

¡Hijole, esto es un supermercado! ¡Todo el mundo viene por su mandado!

Los glóbulos rojos de tu sangre buscan en la papilla todo lo que tu cuerpo necesita para estar saludable.

The waste that your body can't use changes little by little into poop.

Los desechos que tu cuerpo no necesita se transforman poco a poco en bolas de popó.

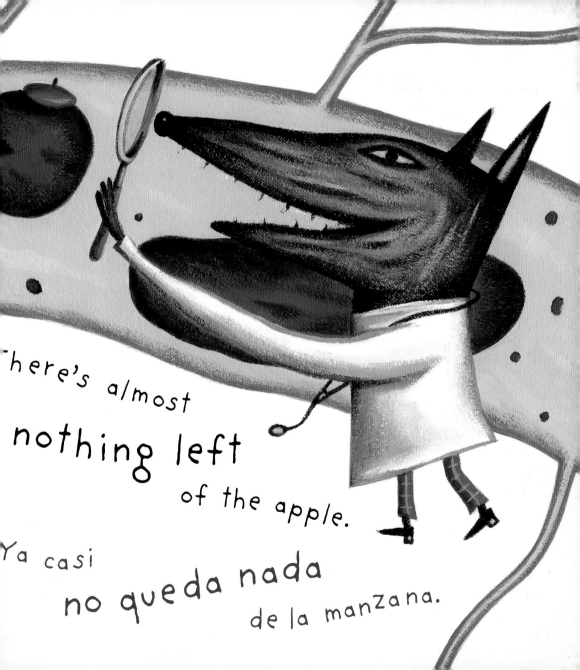

There's almost
nothing left
of the apple.

Ya casi
no queda nada
de la manzana.

Unos músculos especiales empujan la popó hacia el intestino grueso y después hacia el ano.

Special muscles push the poop into the large intestine and then towards your butt.

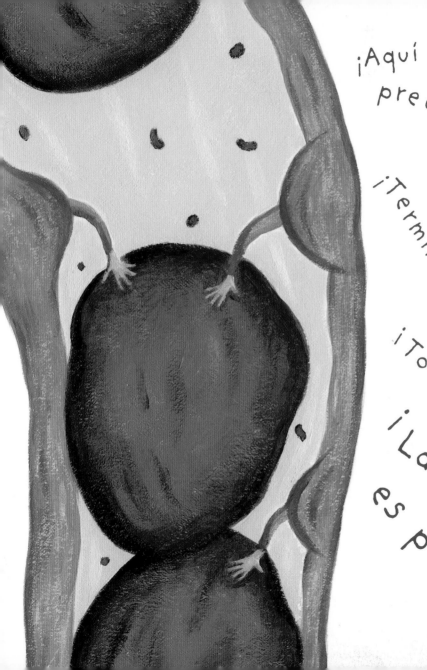

¡Aquí no huele
precisamente
a rosas!

¡Terminó el camino!

¡Todos afuera!

¡La salida
es por aquí!

¿Y si me como otra manzana?

YUM

Siempre es igual. Cada vez que comes algo, el gran viaje del Señor Caca vuelve a empezar.

YUM

Every time, it's the same thing! As soon as you eat something, Mister Poop's long journey begins again.

Originally published in Canada as *Le grand voyage de monsieur Caca*, Les 400 Coups, 2002. Copyright © Angéle Delaunois and Marie Lafrance, 2002.

The Long Journey of Mister Poop / El Gran Viaje del Señor Caca. Translation of the Spanish used with permission of Libros el Nacional. Edit of the Spanish translation by Luis Humberto Crosthwaite. English translation by Daniel Zolinsky copyright 2007 © by Cinco Puntos Press. All rights reserved. No part of this book may be used or reproduced in any manner whatsoever without written consent from the publisher, except for brief quotations for reviews. For further information, write Cinco Puntos Press, 701 Texas Avenue, El Paso, TX 79901; or call 1-915-838-1625.

FIRST EDITION
10   9   8   7   6   5   4   3   2   1

Delaunois, Angéle. [Grand voyage de monsieur Caca. English & Spanish] The long journey of Mister Poop = el gran viaje del Señor Caca / by Angéle Delaunois ; illustrated by Marie Lafrance ; translated by Daniel Zolinsky. — 1st ed.   p. cm.
ISBN-10: 1-933693-07-X / ISBN-13: 978-1-933693-07-1
1. Defecation—Juvenile literature. 2. Digestion—Juvenile literature. I. Lafrance, Marie. II. Title. III. Title: El gran viaje del Señor Caca.
QP159.D45 2007   612.3′6—dc22   2007000968

Cinco Puntos Press

EL PASO, TEXAS

Cover & book design by
Vicki Trego Hill of El Paso, Texas.
Printed in Hong Kong by
Morris Press & Creative Printing, U.S.A.

Visit us at **www.cincopuntos.com** or call 1-800-566-9072